FANTASIA
2000

ISBN 0-634-01610-5

WALT DISNEY MUSIC COMPANY

DISTRIBUTED BY

7777 W. BLUEMOUND RD. P.O. BOX 13819 MILWAUKEE, WI 53213

Disney characters and artwork © Disney Enterprises, Inc.

For all works contained herein:
Unauthorized copying, arranging, adapting, recording or public performance is an infringement of copyright.
Infringers are liable under the law.

Visit Hal Leonard Online at
www.halleonard.com

Contents

Symphony No. 5

Beethoven's **"Symphony No. 5"** serves as the musical springboard for experimentation in moving color and form that advances on the surrealistic and impressionistic "Toccata and Fugue in D Minor" from *Fantasia* in 1940, one of the visual breakthroughs that Walt himself found particularly exciting.

SYMPHONY NO. 5
First Movement

By LUDWIG VAN BEETHOVEN

Allegro con brio

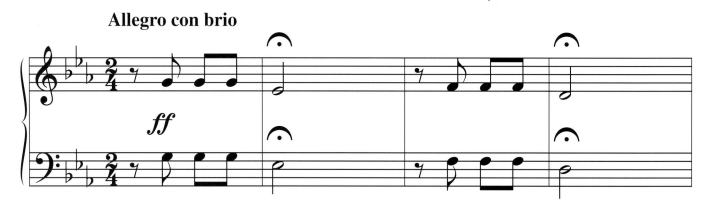

© 2000 Walt Disney Music Company
All Rights Reserved   Used by Permission

cresc.   *f*

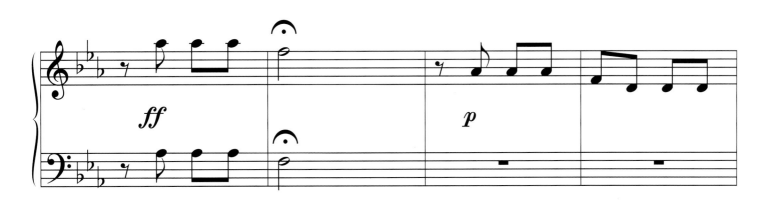

ff

p

cresc.

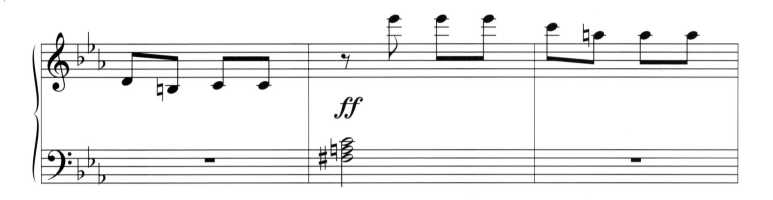

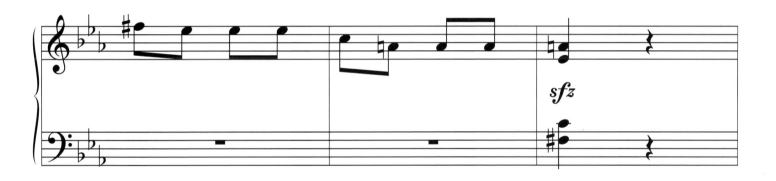

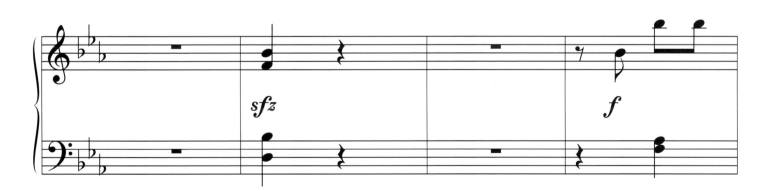

Pines of Rome

For the Disney artists, "**Pines of Rome**" by Respighi did not merely suggest a pedestrian stroll along the Appian Way. Instead, they conjured a family of whales who break free their earthbound restrictions and soar joyously into the sky, as unfettered as their spirits and the animators' imaginations allow them to be.

THE PINES OF THE APPIAN WAY

from PINES OF ROME

OTTORINO RESPIGHI

Tempo di Marcia

Copyright © 1925 by CASA RICORDI - BMG RICORDI S.p.A.
Copyright Renewed
International Copyright Secured   All Rights Reserved

Rhapsody in Blue

The very last sequence to be developed for the *Fantasia/2000* program, **"Rhapsody in Blue,"** happily adds George Gershwin, arguably America's quintessential composer, to the mix of European masters. Additionally, another great American stylist, caricaturist Al Hirschfeld, is celebrated in this interpretation by Director Eric Goldberg set against the backdrop of 1930s Manhattan.

RHAPSODY IN BLUE

Music by GEORGE GERSHWIN

Molto moderato

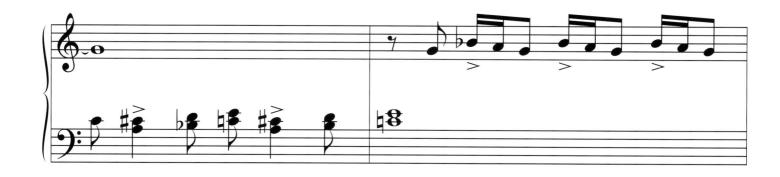

© 1924 WB MUSIC CORP. (Renewed)
GERSHWIN ® and GEORGE GERSHWIN ® are registered trademarks of Gershwin Enterprises
RHAPSODY IN BLUE ® is a trademark of the George Gershwin Family Trust
All Rights Reserved

Grandioso ma non troppo

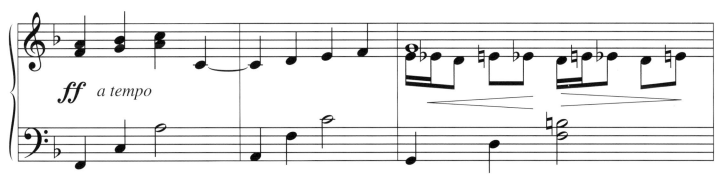

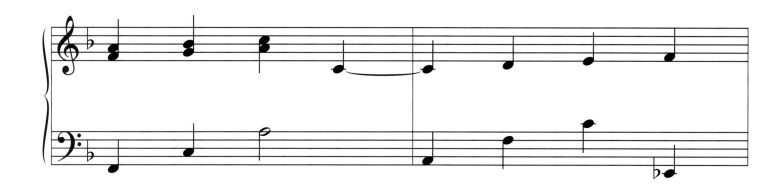

Allargando

There is a memo from late 1940 concerning new numbers for Fantasia in which Walt Disney boldly scrawled in red grease pencil "What about something modern, like Shostakovich?" More than fifty years later Shostakovich and his "**Piano Concerto No. 2, Allegro, Opus 102**" are now a part of *Fantasia/2000*, combined with a story idea that also echoes back to the early Forties when *The Steadfast Tin Soldier* was being developed at Disney's Studio, along with adaptations of several other Hans Christian Andersen stories being planned for a feature film biography of the Danish author. *Fantasia/2000* has linked that Studio heritage with the animator's changing tools of today. Whereas some characters in the sequence are animated by traditional hand-drawn methods, the toys — the Soldier, his ballerina love interest, and the villainous Jack-in-the-Box — are brought to life by the computer as the animator's tool.

PIANO CONCERTO No. 2

First Movement

DMITRI SHOSTAKOVICH
Op. 102

Allegro

Copyright © 1957 (Renewed) by G. Schirmer, Inc. (ASCAP)
International Copyright Secured   All Rights Reserved
Reprinted by Permission

Carnival
of the Animals

Complementing the aural whimsy of the finale from Saint-Saëns' "**Carnival of the Animals**" is the visual delight of frolicking flamingos, one with a yo-yo, whose cavorting is propelled by the flowing watercolor design of animation.

CARNIVAL OF THE ANIMALS
Finale

CAMILLE SAINT-SAËNS

Molto allegro

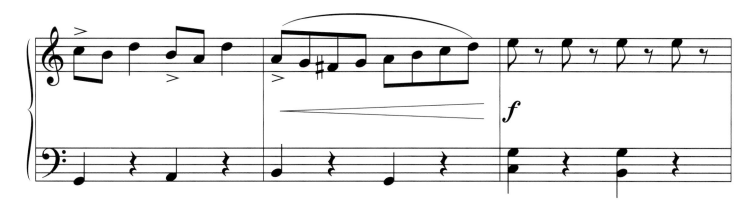

© 2000 Walt Disney Music Company
Original © 1922 Durand S.A. and Used by Permission of Theodore Presser Co.
All Rights Reserved   Used by Permission

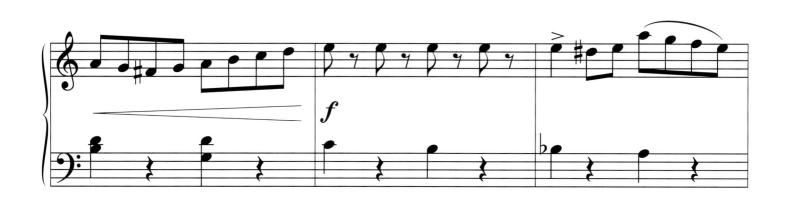

riginally planned as a theatrical short, Dukas' **"The Sorcerer's Apprentice**," the tale of Mickey Mouse's

unfortunate experience with magic gone disastrously out of control, became the catalyst for Walt's development

of *Fantasia* as a feature entirely inspired by classical music. As well as being Mickey's most famous role, the

image of him in his sorcerer's hat, atop a pinnacle and confidently orchestrating the cosmos, has also come to

symbolize the entire initial version of *Fantasia*.

THE SORCERER'S APPRENTICE

PAUL DUKAS

Moderately fast

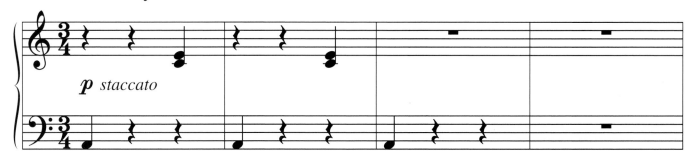

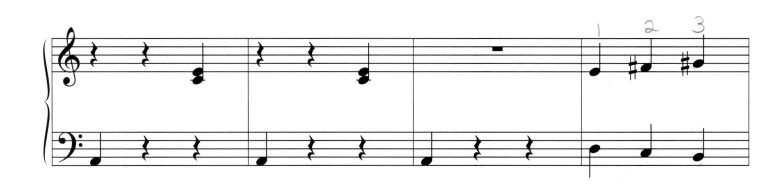

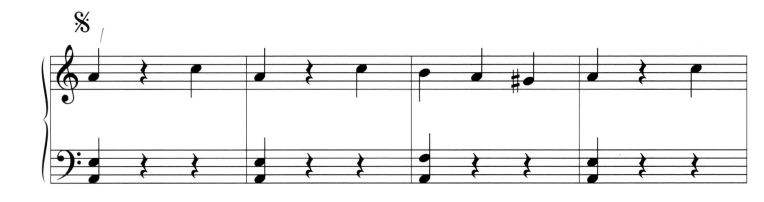

© 2000 Walt Disney Music Company
Original © 1896 Durand S.A. and Used by Permission of Theodore Presser Co.
All Rights Reserved   Used by Permission

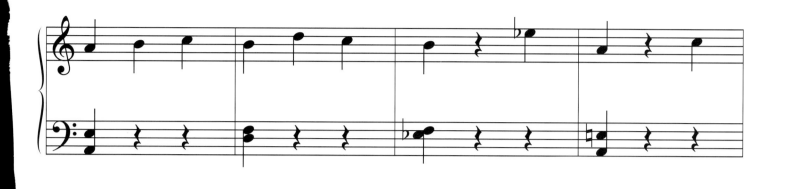

To Coda ⊕

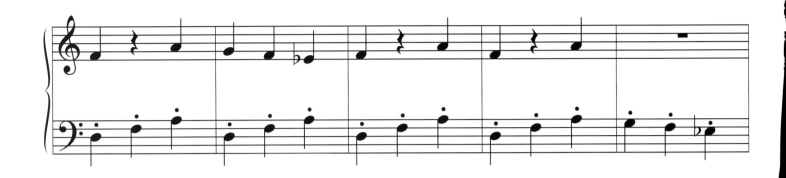

staccato

mp

D.S. al Coda

Coda

f

Pomp and Circumstance

Donald Duck has long shown a tendency to be a bit jealous of his pal Mickey's prominence as a Disney star. (Who can listen to the "Mickey Mouse Club March" without remembering the Duck's insistent insertion of his own name as a counterpoint to the song's repeating "Mickey Mouse" chant?) Now Donald is undoubtedly pleased to share billing with Mickey as the star of his own sequence in *Fantasia/2000* set to music from Elgar's "**Pomp and Circumstance, Marches #1, 2, 3, & 4.**" And not be upstaged by his popular co-star, Donald, too, is confronted by torrents of water on the rampage in his sequence, a duck's-eye account of his experiences aboard Noah's Ark.

POMP AND CIRCUMSTANCE
March No. 1

EDWARD ELGAR

Molto maestoso (♩ = 82)

March No. 1 Original Copyright © 1902 by Boosey & Co.
Copyright Renewed
March No. 4 Original Copyright © 1904 by Boosey & Co.
Copyright Renewed
This arrangement Copyright © 2000 by Boosey & Co. for the world excluding the United States, Canada and Australia
This arrangement © 2000 Walt Disney Music Company for the United States, Canada and Australia
All Rights Reserved   Used by Permission

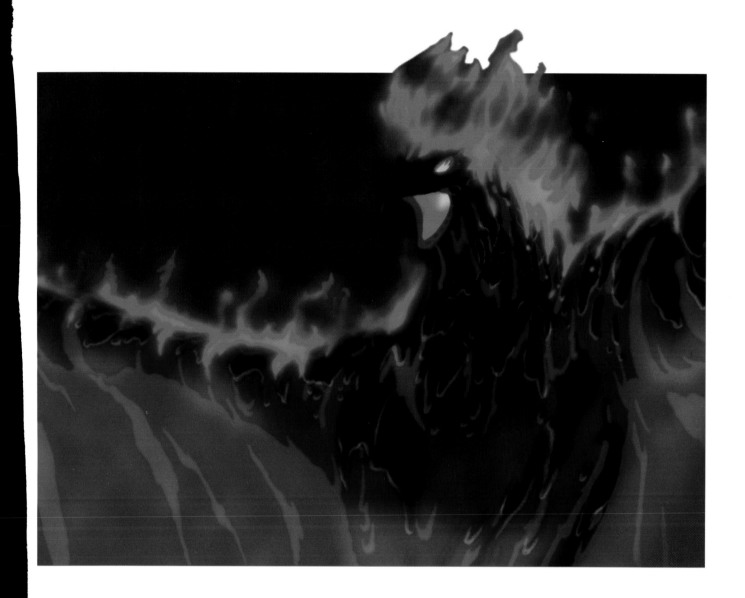

Firebird Suite

Another link to Fantasia's early development is Stravinsky's **"Firebird Suite – 1919 Version."** The selection comprised part of the musical numbers being considered for *Fantasia* in 1938. *Fantasia/2000's* visualization of this piece combines a natural design approach with an art nouveau, fairytale-like look to the animation that soars into unhindered imaginative flight as it flows across the screen.

FIREBIRD SUITE
(1919 Version)

IGOR STRAVINSKY

© 2000 Walt Disney Music Company
All Rights outside the United States Controlled by Schott Musik International, Mainz
All Rights Reserved   Used by Permission

Allegro

sffz *mf*

Lento maestoso

Allegro non troppo